MONEY
affirmations

_____

_____

_____

_____

_____

_____

_____

Savings PLANNER

MONTH	SAVING FOR	AMOUNT

INCOME TRACKER

MONTH OF

DATE	SOURCE	CATEGORY	AMOUNT
		TOTAL	

MONTH OF

DATE	SOURCE	CATEGORY	AMOUNT
		TOTAL	

MONTH OF

DATE	SOURCE	CATEGORY	AMOUNT
		TOTAL	

"

YOU ARE WHAT
YOU BELIVE YOU
you ARE.

- JOSEPH BENNER

I WILL MAKE THIS AMOUNT:

$

ACTION STEPS TO MAKE THIS:

- [ ]
- [ ]
- [ ]
- [ ]

MY MONEY AFFIRMATION:

JANUARY BILLS

DUE DATE	BILL	AMOUNT	PAID
	TOTAL		

Debt PAYMENT TRACKER

BILL:

DATE	BALANCE	PAID	REMAINDER

MONTHLY
Budget Plan

	Month / Years

INCOME

LIST OF INCOME	AMOUNT
1. _____	_____
2. _____	_____
3. _____	_____
TOTAL INCOME	

EXPENSES

BILL & EXPENSES	DUE	AMOUNT
1.		
2.		
3.		
4.		
5.		
6.		
7.		
8.		
9.		
TOTAL INCOME		

TOTAL SAVING

Savings TRACKER

For:

Amount:

Goal date:

Notes

FEBRUARY BILLS

DUE DATE	BILL	AMOUNT	PAID
		TOTAL	

Debt PAYMENT TRACKER

BILL:

DATE	BALANCE	PAID	REMAINDER

MONTHLY
Budget Plan

Month / Years

INCOME

LIST OF INCOME	AMOUNT
1. _____	_____
2. _____	_____
3. _____	_____
TOTAL INCOME	

EXPENSES

BILL & EXPENSES	DUE	AMOUNT
1. _____	_____	_____
2. _____	_____	_____
3. _____	_____	_____
4. _____	_____	_____
5. _____	_____	_____
6. _____	_____	_____
7. _____	_____	_____
8. _____	_____	_____
9. _____	_____	_____
TOTAL INCOME		

TOTAL SAVING

Savings TRACKER

For:

Amount:

Goal date:

Notes

"

THE MOST DIFFICULT
THING
IS THE DECISION TO ACT,
the rest is MERELY
TENACITY

- AMELIA EARHART

I WILL MAKE THIS AMOUNT:

$

ACTION STEPS TO MAKE THIS:

☐ ....
☐ ....
☐ ....
☐ ....

MY MONEY AFFIRMATION:

MARCH BILLS

DUE DATE	BILL	AMOUNT	PAID
		TOTAL	

Debt PAYMENT TRACKER

BILL:

DATE	BALANCE	PAID	REMAINDER

MONTHLY
Budget Plan

Month / Years

INCOME

LIST OF INCOME	AMOUNT
1. _____	_____
2. _____	_____
3. _____	_____
TOTAL INCOME	

EXPENSES

BILL & EXPENSES	DUE	AMOUNT
1. _____	_____	_____
2. _____	_____	_____
3. _____	_____	_____
4. _____	_____	_____
5. _____	_____	_____
6. _____	_____	_____
7. _____	_____	_____
8. _____	_____	_____
9. _____	_____	_____
TOTAL INCOME		

TOTAL SAVING

Savings TRACKER

For:

Amount:

Goal date:

Notes

"

BEWARE OF LITTLE EXPENSES;

A SMALL LEAK WILL SINK A

great SHIP.

- BENJAMIN FRANKLIN

I WILL MAKE THIS AMOUNT:

$

ACTION STEPS TO MAKE THIS:

- ☐ ....
- ☐ ....
- ☐ ....
- ☐ ....

MY MONEY AFFIRMATION:

INCOME TRACKER

MONTH OF

DATE	SOURCE	CATEGORY	AMOUNT
		TOTAL	

MONTH OF

DATE	SOURCE	CATEGORY	AMOUNT
		TOTAL	

MONTH OF

DATE	SOURCE	CATEGORY	AMOUNT
		TOTAL	

APRIL BILLS

DUE DATE	BILL	AMOUNT	PAID
		TOTAL	

Debt PAYMENT TRACKER

BILL: _____

DATE	BALANCE	PAID	REMAINDER

MONTHLY
Budget Plan

Month / Years

INCOME

LIST OF INCOME	AMOUNT
1.	
2.	
3.	
TOTAL INCOME	

EXPENSES

BILL & EXPENSES	DUE	AMOUNT
1.		
2.		
3.		
4.		
5.		
6.		
7.		
8.		
9.		
TOTAL INCOME		

TOTAL SAVING	

Savings TRACKER

For:

Amount: Goal date:

Notes

"

THE BEST THING MONEY CAN BUY IS *financial* FREEDOM.

- ROB BERGER

I WILL MAKE THIS AMOUNT:

$

ACTION STEPS TO MAKE THIS:

☐

....

☐

....

☐

....

☐

....

MY MONEY AFFIRMATION:

MAY BILLS

DUE DATE	BILL	AMOUNT	PAID
		TOTAL	

Debt PAYMENT TRACKER   BILL:

DATE	BALANCE	PAID	REMAINDER

M O N T H L Y
Budget Plan

Month / Years

INCOME

LIST OF INCOME	AMOUNT
1. _____	_____
2. _____	_____
3. _____	_____
TOTAL INCOME	

EXPENSES

BILL & EXPENSES	DUE	AMOUNT
1. _____	_____	_____
2. _____	_____	_____
3. _____	_____	_____
4. _____	_____	_____
5. _____	_____	_____
6. _____	_____	_____
7. _____	_____	_____
8. _____	_____	_____
9. _____	_____	_____
TOTAL INCOME		

TOTAL SAVING

Savings TRACKER

For:

Amount:

Goal date:

Notes

"

EVERY FINANCIAL

DECISION SHOULD BE DRIVEN

BY WHAT

you VALUE.

-David Bacht

I WILL MAKE THIS AMOUNT:

$

ACTION STEPS TO MAKE THIS:

☐

....

☐

....

☐

....

☐

....

MY MONEY AFFIRMATION:

JUNE BILLS

DUE DATE	BILL	AMOUNT	PAID
		TOTAL	

Debt PAYMENT TRACKER

BILL:

DATE	BALANCE	PAID	REMAINDER

MONTHLY
Budget Plan

Month / Years

INCOME

LIST OF INCOME	AMOUNT
1. _____	_____
2. _____	_____
3. _____	_____
TOTAL INCOME	

EXPENSES

BILL & EXPENSES	DUE	AMOUNT
1. _____	_____	_____
2. _____	_____	_____
3. _____	_____	_____
4. _____	_____	_____
5. _____	_____	_____
6. _____	_____	_____
7. _____	_____	_____
8. _____	_____	_____
9. _____	_____	_____
TOTAL INCOME		
TOTAL SAVING		

Savings TRACKER

For:

Amount: Goal date:

Notes

"

TO GET RICH YOU HAVE TO
BE
MAKING MONEY WHILE
you're SLEEP.

- DAVID BAILEY

I WILL MAKE THIS AMOUNT:

$

ACTION STEPS TO MAKE THIS:

- ☐ ....
- ☐ ....
- ☐ ....
- ☐ ....

MY MONEY AFFIRMATION:

INCOME TRACKER

MONTH OF

DATE	SOURCE	CATEGORY	AMOUNT
		TOTAL	

MONTH OF

DATE	SOURCE	CATEGORY	AMOUNT
		TOTAL	

MONTH OF

DATE	SOURCE	CATEGORY	AMOUNT
		TOTAL	

JULY BILLS

DUE DATE	BILL	AMOUNT	PAID
		TOTAL	

Debt PAYMENT TRACKER

BILL:

DATE	BALANCE	PAID	REMAINDER

MONTHLY
Budget Plan

Month / Years

INCOME

LIST OF INCOME	AMOUNT
1. _____	_____
2. _____	_____
3. _____	_____
TOTAL INCOME	

EXPENSES

BILL & EXPENSES	DUE	AMOUNT
1. _____	_____	_____
2. _____	_____	_____
3. _____	_____	_____
4. _____	_____	_____
5. _____	_____	_____
6. _____	_____	_____
7. _____	_____	_____
8. _____	_____	_____
9. _____	_____	_____
TOTAL INCOME		

TOTAL SAVING	

$\mathcal{Savings}$ TRACKER

For:

Amount:

Goal date:

Notes

"

DON'T COMPARE YOUR

BEGINNING TO SOMEONE

else's MIDDLE.

- JON ACUFF

I WILL MAKE THIS AMOUNT:

$

ACTION STEPS TO MAKE THIS:

- [ ] ....
- [ ] ....
- [ ] ....
- [ ] ....

MY MONEY AFFIRMATION:

AUGUST BILLS

DUE DATE	BILL	AMOUNT	PAID
		TOTAL	

Debt PAYMENT TRACKER

BILL:

DATE	BALANCE	PAID	REMAINDER

M O N T H L Y
Budget Plan

Month / Years

INCOME

LIST OF INCOME	AMOUNT
1. _____	_____
2. _____	_____
3. _____	_____
TOTAL INCOME	

EXPENSES

BILL & EXPENSES	DUE	AMOUNT
1. _____	_____	_____
2. _____	_____	_____
3. _____	_____	_____
4. _____	_____	_____
5. _____	_____	_____
6. _____	_____	_____
7. _____	_____	_____
8. _____	_____	_____
9. _____	_____	_____
TOTAL INCOME		

TOTAL SAVING

$\mathcal{S}avings$ TRACKER

For:

Amount:

Goal date:

Notes

I WILL MAKE THIS AMOUNT:

$

ACTION STEPS TO MAKE THIS:

☐
....
☐
....
☐
....
☐
....

MY MONEY AFFIRMATION:

SEPTEMBER BILLS

DUE DATE	BILL	AMOUNT	PAID
		TOTAL	

Debt PAYMENT TRACKER

BILL:

DATE	BALANCE	PAID	REMAINDER

MONTHLY
Budget Plan

Month / Years

INCOME

LIST OF INCOME	AMOUNT
1.	
2.	
3.	
TOTAL INCOME	

EXPENSES

BILL & EXPENSES	DUE	AMOUNT
1.		
2.		
3.		
4.		
5.		
6.		
7.		
8.		
9.		
TOTAL INCOME		
TOTAL SAVING		

Savings TRACKER

For:

Amount:

Goal date:

Notes

"

YOU DON'T HAVE TO SEE

THE WHOLE STAIRCASE,

just the first **STEP.**

- MARTIN LUTHER KING,
JR.

I WILL MAKE THIS AMOUNT:

$

ACTION STEPS TO MAKE THIS:

☐
....
☐
....
☐
....
☐
....

MY MONEY AFFIRMATION:

MONTH OF

DATE	SOURCE	CATEGORY	AMOUNT
		TOTAL	

MONTH OF

DATE	SOURCE	CATEGORY	AMOUNT
		TOTAL	

MONTH OF

DATE	SOURCE	CATEGORY	AMOUNT
		TOTAL	

OCTOBER BILLS

DUE DATE	BILL	AMOUNT	PAID
		TOTAL	

Debt PAYMENT TRACKER

BILL:

DATE	BALANCE	PAID	REMAINDER

MONTHLY
Budget Plan

Month / Years

INCOME

LIST OF INCOME	AMOUNT
1. _____	_____
2. _____	_____
3. _____	_____
TOTAL INCOME	

EXPENSES

BILL & EXPENSES	DUE	AMOUNT
1. _____	_____	_____
2. _____	_____	_____
3. _____	_____	_____
4. _____	_____	_____
5. _____	_____	_____
6. _____	_____	_____
7. _____	_____	_____
8. _____	_____	_____
9. _____	_____	_____
TOTAL INCOME		

TOTAL SAVING	

Savings TRACKER

For:

Amount:

Goal date:

Notes

"

IF YOU TAKE CONTROL OF
YOUR FINANCES TODAY,

THEN YOU WON'T BE A
VICTIM
of THEM
TOMMOROW.

- EMILY G. STROUD

I WILL MAKE THIS AMOUNT:

$

ACTION STEPS TO MAKE THIS:

☐

....

☐

....

☐

....

☐

....

MY MONEY AFFIRMATION:

NOVEMBER BILLS

DUE DATE	BILL	AMOUNT	PAID
		TOTAL	

Debt PAYMENT TRACKER   BILL:

DATE	BALANCE	PAID	REMAINDER

MONTHLY
Budget Plan

Month / Years

INCOME

LIST OF INCOME	AMOUNT
1. _____	_____
2. _____	_____
3. _____	_____
TOTAL INCOME	

EXPENSES

BILL & EXPENSES	DUE	AMOUNT
1. _____	_____	_____
2. _____	_____	_____
3. _____	_____	_____
4. _____	_____	_____
5. _____	_____	_____
6. _____	_____	_____
7. _____	_____	_____
8. _____	_____	_____
9. _____	_____	_____
TOTAL INCOME		

TOTAL SAVING

$\mathcal{Savings}$ TRACKER

For:

Amount:

Goal date:

Notes

"

DO NOT SAVE

but spend

WHAT IS LEFT AFTER SPENDING, BUT
SPEND WHAT IS LEFT AFTER

SAVING

- WARREN BUFFETT

I WILL MAKE THIS AMOUNT:

$

ACTION STEPS TO MAKE THIS:

- [ ] ....
- [ ] ....
- [ ] ....
- [ ] ....

MY MONEY AFFIRMATION:

DECEMBER BILLS

DUE DATE	BILL	AMOUNT	PAID
		TOTAL	

Debt PAYMENT TRACKER

BILL:

DATE	BALANCE	PAID	REMAINDER

MONTHLY
Budget Plan

Month / Years

INCOME

LIST OF INCOME	AMOUNT
1. _____	_____
2. _____	_____
3. _____	_____
TOTAL INCOME	

EXPENSES

BILL & EXPENSES	DUE	AMOUNT
1. _____	_____	_____
2. _____	_____	_____
3. _____	_____	_____
4. _____	_____	_____
5. _____	_____	_____
6. _____	_____	_____
7. _____	_____	_____
8. _____	_____	_____
9. _____	_____	_____
TOTAL INCOME		

TOTAL SAVING

Savings TRACKER

For:

Amount:

Goal date:

Notes